Y0-DDO-809

THE POWER OF ESSENTIAL OILS

Everything You Need to Know about Essential Oils

LUIS ANGEL FRANCO

The Power of Essential Oils

Everything You Need to Know about Essential Oils

Table of Contents

Introduction

Do you know what essential oils are? Do you know what they can do for you? If you are like many, you think they are a new phenomenon thought up in the 21st century as a new method of holistic medicine. That's not at all true though. In fact, as you will learn in the first part of this book, essential oils and the idea of aromatherapy have been around for thousands and thousands of years. People have known for a very long time what they could do.

These days, the oils have become so well-known and so scientifically studied that they are being used in conjunction with traditional medicine. That certainly means a lot of people believe in them.

The purpose of this book is to tell you everything you need to know about essential oils, and it has been broken down into sections.

In the first section, we will discuss essential oils in general. The last section will provide you with further resources and information that you will need to know. It even includes an extensive list of essential oil recipes that you can use for yourself or even to clean your home.

So, are you ready to put aside any preconceived notions you may have had about essential oils and then learn what they truly are?

If so, then let's get started with section one of this book…

Part I: Essential Oils

Chapter 1:

The History

Essential oils have been in use for a very long time, dating way back to Biblical times. They are not a new concept even though they have not always been called essential oils specifically.

Because they are so powerful and have been used for so long, this certainly should be cause enough for you to understand how they could help in your own life. So, before we get into details about the oils themselves, let's look at the history for as far back as we have record. (It's entirely probable that they were around for even longer, but we don't have written records to detail it.)

Ancient Egypt

From the historical records and information that we have, essential oils were used as far back as the ancient Egyptians. This society was very far advanced in many fields, so it is no wonder that they were some of the first people to understand how to extract and use the oils.

"The ancient Egyptians believed that the sense of smell and the ability to detect odors was the most important of our sensory abilities. They considered the sense of smell far more important than sight or even the ability to think. That was because they knew the importance of odors to increase our intrinsic 'frequency' and transform us." (Hauck)

Because aromatherapy was so important to the ancient Egyptians, they used it in numerous different ways, including:

- Religious Ceremonies

- Cosmetics

- Medicines

- Embalming

The Egyptians used an extraction method called enfleurage to get the essential oil and there are examples of distillation pots dating back to 3,500 BC.

Ancient Greece

If we move forward in time to the ancient Greeks, we will see that the power of essential oils had evolved to take over a great deal of medical treatments. We know from history that Greece focused a great deal on medical wisdom. For example, Hippocrates was considered one of the greatest physicians of ancient times.

Hippocrates, as well as other Greek physicians, began using holistic treatments to manage a variety of different illnesses and conditions. Aromatherapy was used in the treatment itself and holistic massage as well.

The Far East

In countries like China and India, essential oils became the base of their medicinal treatments and they continue to play a very important role in Eastern medicine. During the same time that the ancient Greeks were using aromatherapy in treatments, the Chinese were using aromatic plants to provide medicines. Additionally, the Indian medicinal system called Ayurveda is based strongly on the use of essential oils.

The Roman Empire

The Roman Empire depended greatly on the research and beliefs of the Greeks. So, it is no wonder that they continued the use of essential oils. However, the Romans took things a step further. They believed that essential oils could be used to maintain good hygiene as well as overall good health. They believed very strongly that aromatherapy could be used to not just treat conditions, but also to ensure health problems never arose.

The Biblical Times

The Bible actually mentions the use of oils more than 100 times throughout the Old and New Testaments. Some of the scriptures that mention various oils include:

- Aloes – Numbers 24:6, Proverbs 7:17, Song of Solomon 4:14, and John 19:39.

- Cassia – Exodus 30:24, Psalm 45:8

- Cedarwood – The Book of Leviticus and Numbers 19:6

- Cypress – Genesis 6:14, Isaiah 44:14, I Kings 9:11, Song of Solomon 1:17

- Frankincense – Mentioned throughout Exodus, Leviticus, Numbers, I Chronicles, Nehemiah, Song of Solomon, Isaiah, Jeremiah, Matthew, and Revelation.

- Galbanum – Exodus 31:24

- Hyssop – Exodus 12: 22, Numbers 19:6. Psalm 51:7, Hebrews 9:19

- Myrrh – Mentioned throughout Genesis, Exodus, Esther, Psalm, Proverbs, Song of Solomon, Matthew, Mark, John, and Revelation.

- Rose of Sharon – Song of Solomon 2:1

The Bible makes it very clear that essential oils have been used for a very long time, dating almost all the way back to creation.

The Renaissance

For a while, after the ancient times, the use of essential oils began to almost die away. The only way it survived the Dark Ages was through monasteries that continued to use the oils for treatments and medicinal purposes. During the Dark Ages, people who discussed the use of herbs were often considered witches and were even persecuted.

Then came the Renaissance when the Western World managed to rise out of the Dark Ages and begin moving toward modernization. Many physicians began using essential oils once again during this time period. This was spurred by one doctor named Paracelsus, who believed there was much to be found in folk wisdom.

In fact, even though doctors at this time were considered absurd for their use of aromatherapy, they came to be well recognized for their success in curing otherwise debilitating conditions like leprosy.

The use of essential oils continued at some level for many hundreds of years until the modern time, when they gained their name and became a worldwide phenomenon. For a long time in the past, they were even considered the main form of medicine. As modern medicine began to develop, essential oils took on a new role, as a supporter so to speak. For that reason, they began to be thought of as "alternative" medicine. It has only been in the modern day that people have been able to truly see how this alternative medicine and traditional medicine can work together hand-in-hand.

So, in the next chapter, let's look at how aromatherapy and folk medicine led to the essential oils we can now use thanks to a series of doctors, researchers, and discoveries.

Chapter 2:

The Modern Aromatherapy

Now, let's move from talking about aromatherapy and essential oils in the ancient times and discuss how they have evolved into what they are now. It took several steps and decades for this to happen. Even though aromatherapy has gone through times when it just was not as popular as others, it has never completely disappeared. To see this, let's look at a timeline.

Beginning with Flower Therapy

One of the pioneers of modern essential oils and aromatherapy was Dr. Edward Bach around the turn of the 20th century. He was a physician and pathologist with a background in bacteriology as well. Over the years, he learned that orthodox medicine did not always seem to work and he got tired of patients undergoing treatments to no avail.

So, he started seeking other types of treatments that focused on helping a patient treat their personality instead of the condition itself. This included something he referred to as flower therapy. He used various derivatives of flowers and plants to help effect a personality for the better.

While the work that Bach did was not accepted at the time and other doctors indicated it showed no logic, he did manage to have extremely good results with his therapies.

Rene Maurice Gattefosse

Around 1937, Rene Maurice Gattefosse actually coined the modern term we use, aromatherapy. He didn't exactly believe in natural and alternative medicines, but he found that there was something to essential oils that traditional medicine could not explain. It all began in 1910, when he burned his own hand. Because the burn was very painful, he grabbed for the first thing available, which happened to be undiluted essential oil of lavender. Gattefosse noticed immediately that the lavender soothed the pain from the burn. Then, as the hand began to heal, he even noticed that it healed more quickly and he wasn't even left with a scar. Fascinated, he began experimenting with essential oils, and he found:

- Very small amounts of these essential oils could interact with the chemistry of the body and could even be absorbed through the skin.

- Essential oils could help injuries heal. In fact, with Gattefosse's experiments, a doctor named Jean Valet found that he could use different essential oils to treat wounds of soldiers during World War II.

Because of his discoveries, essential oils were carried on into the modern day.

Marguerite Maury

Maury lived during the 1950s, and she combined information that Gattefosse found along with Tibetan methods of using essential oils. As a result, she created a technique of combining essential oils with vegetable oils as a carrier and then massaging them into the skin along the spine of the back so that the oils soaked into the nerves.

Marguerite Maury didn't stop there either. She began prescribing essential oils on an individual basis determined by each patient's needs. She would offer various combinations of essential oils to each patient so that the person could be properly massaged to treat their own conditions.

Because so many people were finding essential oils so helpful, the techniques began to take on speed. Soon, aromatherapy and essential oils became a staple in holistic health methods. The true modern movement began in the late 1970s and has not slowed down since then. In the 21st century, these oils are not just used by those who subscribe to holistic medicines either. In fact, the uses and treatments in medications and other therapies are preferred by people of all types.

You may just be surprised at the many different modern uses for essential oils too. Different mixes and combinations can be used for:

- Bathing and Relaxation

- Compresses for Pain Relief

- Foot and Hand Care

- Hair Care

- Massages

- Sitz Bath Treatments

- Inhalers and Vaporizers

- Skin Care

- Saunas and Jacuzzis

- And More

We will talk about the uses in further depth later in this book. However, before we do anything else, it's important that you learn the basics of the oils so that you will get started correctly. In fact, in the third section of this book, you will even find recipes you can use to make these essential oil product. However, let's save that for later.

Chapter 3:

Essential Oil Basics

Now, before you really get started with essential oils, you do need to learn the basics of them. Here is a basic definition of what they are:

> "Essential oils are natural compounds that are found in the seeds, bark, rinds, stems, roots, flowers, and other parts of plants. They always come from the liferoot of the plant. They give plants, flowers, fruit their aromatic smell and are therefore heavily used in aromatherapy." (EO Basics)

The process of making essential oils uses steam distillation so that the oils will separate from the plants. The steam mixture circulates throughout the plant and the whole process is kept under pressure. Then, when the whole thing is cooled down, the steam and oil mixture turns into liquid. Of course, the steam is water and it will not stay mixed with oil. The two will separate and this allows the collection of essential oils in the most pure, concentrated form.

Facts About Essential Oils

Here are some interesting facts about the oils and what they can do. You may be surprised at what it takes to get the oils and what they are capable of doing for people who use them.

- To get about 5 mL of rose essential oils, it takes the use of about 12,000 roses.

- Essential oil is not the same as oil (as in canola or corn). While they are not water based, they also don't have fatty lipids found in cooking oils. These essential oils absorb into the skin immediately.

- A scientific study was completed and found that one type of essential oil blend can actually kill the influenza virus.

- A vast majority of essential oils have antibacterial properties and that makes them great for household cleaners.

- There is a difference between flavoring, fragrance oil and essential oil. The first two won't offer the benefits of the latter.

- There are dangers to essential oils. We will discuss the dangers as well as safe use later in this guide.

- Essential oils last a very long time. One bottle can last anywhere from 5 to 10 years depending on their type.

Now, are you ready to delve in the good stuff and learn the different types of essential oils available and what they can do? Let's get to it.

Types of Essential Oils

Below is a list of all the essential oils as well as those not sold or legally allowed in the United States. It's important that you understand the options before you begin choosing. It's also important that you avoid those oils that are not sold in the country for specific reasons (they could be dangerous). In part III of this book, you will also find a full list of dangerous or toxic essential oils that you should avoid at all costs.

Essential Oils	Essential Oils	Not Available in U.S.	Carrier Oils*
Allspice	Niaouli	Angelica	Almond
Aniseed	Nutmeg	Birch	Aloe Vera
Basil	Orange	Bitter Almond	Apricot Kernel

Bay	Palma Rosa	Boldo	Avocado
Benzoin	Patchouli	Buchu	Calendula
Bergamot	Peppermint	Cardamom	Evening Primrose
Black Pepper	Petitgrain	Cumin	Grape Seed
Cajaput	Pimento	Elemi	Hazelnut
Calamus	Pine	Mugwart	Jojoba
Camomile	Rose	Mustard	Macadamia
Camphor	Rose Geranium	Oregano	Olive
Caraway	Rosemary	Pennyroyal	Sesame
Carrot Seed	Rosewood	Rose Otto	Walnut
Cassia	Sage	Rue	Wheatgerm
Cedarwood	Sandalwood	Sassafras	
Cinnamon	Spearmint	Tansy	**Carriers not Available in U.S.**
Citronella	Spikenard	Tarragon	Pumpkin Seed
Clary Sage	Targetes	Savin	Safflower
Clove	Tangerine	Thuja	Sunflower
Coriander	Thyme	Tuberose	

Cypress	Tea Tree	Vanilla	
Dill	Vetiver	Wintergreen	
Eucalyptus	Ylang-Ylang	Wormseed	
Fennel		Wormwood	
Frenkincense		Yarrow	
Geranium			
Ginger			
Grapefruit			
Helichrysum			
Hyssop			
Lavender			
Lemon			
Lemongress			
Lemon Verbena			
Lime			
Mandarin			* Carrier Oils are Used to Dilute the Essential Oils for Safe Use
Marjoram			
Myrrh			

Neroli			

As you can see, there are numerous different types of essential oils available for use in different ways.

Chapter 4:

Uses for These Oils, Do They Work?

There are essentially unlimited different ways you could use essential oils for your mind and body as well as for cleaning and much, much more.

Uses

It would be impossible to list all of the uses, so here are some of the most popular options.

- Peppermint is a very popular essential oil because it can be used in so many different ways. It adds a nice aroma to cleaning products. It can be used to help stave off acne and oily skin problems. It can even be used in lip balms. Some people have found that if they rub a little peppermint oil on their wrists, the aroma can help them stay awake.

- Rosemary is ideal for use with various hair products as well as to cleanse oily and acne prone skin.

- Lemon is very versatile. It can be used in cleaning products and you will enjoy the refreshing scent it leaves behind. It can even be used to tone skin and works well as an aromatherapy mood lifter. Lemon also works well as a mosquito repellent.

- Sweet Orange is another versatile option (are you beginning to see that there are so many uses?). With this, you can create a room spray that is actually calming for people. It can be used as a skin treatment as well.

- Lavender is well-known for its relaxation power. It works well for aromatherapy and can be used in bath products as well to enjoy the relaxing qualities. Some people have even found lavender works great as a topical treatment for irritations like mosquito bites. Of course, as mentioned in the history of the oils, lavender works well for burns.

- Rose Geranium can be used to create perfumes and body sprays as well as in homemade moisturizer.

- Tea Tree Oil is a versatile oil that can help heal injuries, fight acne, and stave off bacteria. Tea Tree Oil is recommended for a variety of different skin problems and even to help heal piercings and other damage. Tea Tree oil can be used in certain types of colognes and body sprays.

- Clove and Cinnamon essential oils are fantastic as room fresheners and offer an amazing scent when used in this way. Additionally, Cinnamon oil can even be used to polish wood furnishings.

- Chamomile is already well-known as a relaxant, and you can add a couple of drops of the oil right on your bed pillow so that you will sleep more easily at night.

This list could go on and on, so it will be your job to find out what essential oils could help you in your daily life with either home chores or your physical and mental wellbeing.

Science of the Oils

Because essential oils have become so popular, there have been numerous research studies into the science behind this alternative medicine. As more research has been done, more has been learned about the power of these oils. Some of the trials that have been completed indicate that essential oils can:

- Some preliminary trials have found that certain types of essential oils, including lavender, have been effective in calming patients who have Alzheimer's disease or other types of dementia.

- A lotion including lemon even helped to calm agitation in patients with severe dementia.

- A third study found that geranium was able to ease anxiety in Alzheimer's patients as well.

- A study on cigarette addiction found that black pepper essential oils can help to reduce the cravings felt by people who are trying to quit smoking.

- A few preliminary studies have shown that peppermint oil, when applied topically, could help ease tension headaches.

- A study that addressed the issue of anxiety worked with more than 100 patients waiting to see a dentist. They found that patients who inhaled lavender scents were calmer than those who did not.

- A study of clary, lavender, and rose found that a mix of these oils can be massaged on the abdominal region and actually help to reduce the problems of menstrual pain.

(Aromatherapy)

This is just the beginning of the studies too. However, it is important to keep in mind that these trials and studies are in their very preliminary phases and nothing concrete has been found by the scientific and medical world. The more these oils are studied, it's likely there will be even more scientific evidence to back up their abilities. So, if you want to find out more, keep watching the news and continue to keep abreast of essential oil updates specifically. You may just be surprised what scientists find in the coming years.

There is a reference listed in the further resources section that you can use if you would like to find out more about the scientific backing of essential oils. This resource is called PubMed. The website is designed to create and combine a variety of different medical and scientific studies, trials, and findings. This way, anyone can see what types of studies have been completed and what information is available to be read. To read and research, just go to the PubMed website and type in "essential oils" in the search bar. This will give you immediate results to academic papers that focus on the findings of trials and studies on essential oils.

Of course, you don't have to read all of that scientific information if you don't want to. It can be very in-depth. However, whether you plan on just using the oils or you would like to sell them to others, it is very important that you understand what they are capable of and what has been proven about them so far.

Think about this. If you are met with a potential customer who is a skeptic, they may be very wary of even considering essential oils. That means you will need to convince them that they do work. If you have scientific information that points to the power of essential oils, then this will definitely mean the skeptic has to rethink their standing. If you plan on selling the oils, you have to know what you are talking about and that may mean doing research. So, learn as much as you can and you will continue to see how powerful the oils can be.

Now that you know much more about the basics of essential oils and you have seen some of the many ways they can be used, let's move on to the in-depth questions you may have along with helpful and detailed answers.

Chapter 5:

Questions Answered

Before you can really get started with essential oils, there are quite a few different questions you need answered. Remember that if they aren't used in the proper way, the oils can be dangerous. Additionally, if you don't know what to look for when choosing them, you may not get the oils you want or need, or they may come to you in a very diluted and unhelpful form. So, let's answer some questions about the power and use of essential oils.

Does It Matter Where the Oils Come From?

Some people may think that an essential oil will be exactly the same as long as it came from the right plant and it is undiluted. However, that is not the case. The quality of the oils begins where it is farmed and how the plants are grown. Healthy soil will mean a healthy plant, and that means a better quality essential oil. In fact, there are things that could be done during farming that may have a massively negative impact on the quality of the oils:

- The use of pesticides and herbicides on the plants

- The surrounding climate and controlled growth of the plants

- The soil quality (soil that is worn out or overworked will not produce quality plants)

It is very important where the essential oils come from, so ordering some off-brand that you found for a really low cost will likely be a big mistake. You won't get that quality unless you do your research and find the right growers and providers of essential oils.

How Much of Each Plant Does It Take to Make Different Concentrations?

There is actually very little of the pure oil in each plant and that means a surprising quantity of plants are needed to create even a small amount of essential oils. So, that is something to think about when considering price. Here are some prices and yields for essential oils:

- 2000-5000 pounds of rose petals will create one pound of essential oil.

- 1000 pounds of jasmine will create a pound of essential oil (that's about 3 million flowers!).

- 200 pounds of lavender flowers will create one pound of essential oil.

As you can see, it takes a massive amount of plants, stems, flowers, bark, or rinds to create even a small amount of essential oil.

Why Is It Important to Follow Instructions?

When you choose essential oils, it is very, very important to follow instructions. In the next chapter, we will discuss safety, but what you must keep in mind is that these oils are undiluted and that means they are very strong. If you use them improperly, you may not get the results from them you want. Additionally, they could become dangerous and cause reactions, amongst other things.

Some essential oils are made to be used undiluted while others need to be diluted. Some can be added to food and beverages while others should never be consumed. If you don't follow the instructions, you could be putting yourself in danger.

How Long Do Essential Oils Last?

As mentioned before, if you take care of the oils, they can last a long time. That doesn't mean forever though. Generally, with proper care, they can last from 5 to 10 years. However, there are a lot of variables in their shelf lives. For example, citrus oils tend to spoil quickly (between one and three years) while bark based or woodsy oils can easily last eight years. Here are some tips on making sure your oils last as long as possible:

- Keep the bottles out of direct sunlight. It's best to keep them in a dark cabinet.

- Keep the bottles as cool as possible. Preferably you should store them in a refrigerator or wine cabinet.

- Make sure you always close lids tightly after each use of the oils.

You also need to know the signs that the oils are going bad. If the oils begin to look cloudy, become a lot thicker or smell strange, then this is a sign it is time to get rid of them.

Do I Need a Diffuser?

You don't technically need a diffuser to enjoy aromatherapy from essential oils. Although, it can be very helpful. You can even use small car diffusers too. There are also many different ways you can use essential oils without a diffuser, such as in bath and body products or cleaning tools.

Where Can I Find Recipes for Essential Oils?

Because essential oils are everywhere, recipes are too. You can find them all over the Internet. Additionally, many companies that sell the oils will even help you determine signature mixes that will help you personally. You will also find a whole variety of recipes in the third section of this book.

Are There People Who Shouldn't Use Essential Oils?

There are some situations where you do need to be especially careful, and we will talk more about that in the next chapter. However, the short answer is women who are pregnant and people who have asthma or certain skin conditions should consult a physician before using the oils, just to be safe.

Are All Essential Oils Certified Safe?

Not necessarily. This depends wholly on the company from which you buy. Some companies do put their oils through rigorous and scientific tests that ensure they really are certified safe. We will talk more about one of those companies later in this book.

However, there are some companies that will slap just any label on their product to make things look better. Just because you see something on a label doesn't mean you can take it as gospel, so be very careful to do your research and find a trustworthy company from the beginning.

Why Do Some Essential Oil Brands Smell Better Than Others?

This has a lot to do with purity. Many companies cut their essential oils with carrier oils just to save money. After all, the pure oils are not cheap. They will do this and then label their oils 100% pure, but this is misleading. They are certainly 100% pure of whatever they include. That may be pure jojoba oil as well as essential oil though.

Brands like dōTERRA that do offer truly pure oils are going to smell better. That's because the only aroma you are getting is the essential oil itself.

Are All Essential Oils Organic?

Unfortunately, no. Many companies are not careful with how they source their oils and the result could contain pesticides and other chemical residues. dōTERRA is one of the few companies that does offer organic oils. While they are not certified, that doesn't mean anything. The oils are sourced from a variety of different companies, states, and provinces. The rules around organic change from one place to another. So, it would be nearly impossible to certify every single thing. However, companies like dōTERRA do ensure their oils are pure, organic, and chemical free.

So, with all of those questions answered, you are one step closer to knowing what you need to about essential oils. Let's move on to the next chapter and discuss safety because this is extremely important. Essential oils can be dangerous if you don't use them properly, so you need to understand safety measures and that way you will simply enjoy all of the benefits.

Chapter 6:

Understanding How to Be Safe When Using Essential Oils

Some people see the words "organic" or "natural" and they immediately assume that a product is safe. However, that is not necessarily the case. Essential oils are pure, undiluted plant oils. They can be very severe or harsh on the skin and they can be downright dangerous in some situations. The only way you can use the oils safely and enjoy their benefits is to understand how to use them properly.

First, I want to say don't be afraid. Just because essential oils can be dangerous, doesn't mean they can't be useful. You just need to know what you are doing and always follow directions. So, let's talk about how you can be safe when using essential oils.

What to Avoid

If you have certain medical conditions, there are also certain essential oils that you need to avoid. That's because they could interact with your medication or even your condition itself. These include:

- If you have diabetes, avoid the use of angelica.

- If you have epilepsy, avoid essential oils that can stimulate the nervous system, including rosemary, fennel, and sage.

- If you have high blood pressure, you should avoid rosemary, sage, thyme, and hyssop.

- If you are pregnant, you should be careful with any essential oils and always discuss their use with your doctor or an experienced aromatherapist. You should avoid certain oils at all costs during pregnancy, and they include juniper, citronella, aniseed, cumin, thyme, angelica, laurel, and basil.

- If you have sensitive skin, you will need to be careful when using oils in any type of topical treatment. The ones that are most commonly associated with sensitive skin irritation include: lemongrass, lemon, jasmine, ginger, citronella, lemon balm, chamomile, yarrow, mint, geranium, coriander, tea tree, basil, laurel, and neroli. Before you use any essential oil, even those not listed, be sure to rub a little on the inside of your wrist to see if you have an allergic reaction.

If you have a medical condition and you are still interested in essential oils, then it is a good idea to talk to a doctor as well as a licensed, experienced aromatherapist. This way, you can make sure you aren't doing anything that could be dangerous.

Additionally, there are some drug interactions you should note so that you can ensure your safety when using essential oils.

Certain essential oils have a sedative like effect and when they are combined with sedative medications, this could put you at risk, especially if you are driving or using any type of machinery. The sedative medications that you should not use sedative essential oils with include:

- Ambien

- Klonopin

- Ativan

- Donnatal

- Others

Peppermint oil specifically has also shown some drug interactions to note. They include:

- Peppermint oil could slow the absorption rate of any prescription drug. Check with your physician before using it.

- The essential oil may cause drugs that include isoenzyme for intestinal conditions to not metabolize properly.

- Peppermint oil does not mix well with felodipine, which is a medication for hypertension. It seems the oil prevents the medication from metabolizing as it should.

If you are on any of these medications or any prescription medications at all, it is very important that you discuss with your physician if it is safe for you to use the oils.

Why Dilution Is Important

Some people selling essential oils may try to tell you that you should not dilute them, but this is never ever the case. In fact, you should always dilute to be safe.

> "Dose is the most important factor in essential oil safety. Some essential oils used in the wrong doses or too high a concentration have been found (in animals and laboratory studies) to contribute to tumor development and other harmful changes in the body. Some undiluted essential oils can even be damaging to the skin, liver, and other organs if used improperly." (Are Essential Oils Safe?)

If you do not dilute the oils, you could face serious skin damage and possibly even skin cancer. For example, bergamot, lemon, lime, angelica, and orange all cause photo sensitivity, which means your skin is more sensitive to the sun and more prone to cancer.

Again, don't be scared away from essential oils because of this. They can be extremely beneficial. You just need to make sure you are diluting them properly before you use them.

Children and Essential Oils

Not all essential oils are safe for children, and the ones that are should be used in a very diluted manner. That's because children are more sensitive than adults and can be more prone to adverse reactions.

There are three main oils that are safe for use with children, and you can remember them by thinking TLC.

T – Tea Tree Oil

L – Lavender

C – Chamomile

You can use those oils as room fresheners, compresses for injuries, and bathing. The list of oils that are simply too strong for use with children includes:

Basil	Clove	Lemon Verbena	Red Thyme
Bay	Costus	Lemongrass	All toxic essential oils
Benzoin	Cumin	Nutmeg	
Bergamot	Eucalyptus	Orange	
Birch	Fennel	Oregano	

Black Pepper	Fir	Parsley Seed	
Cassia	Ginger	Peppermint	
Cedarwood	Helichrysum	Pimento	
Cinnamon	Juniper	Pine	
Citronella	Lemon	Tagetes	

If you choose to use any of these with your children, make sure you do so with extreme caution. Always dilute them extensively and follow the advice of your aromatherapist.

Other things you need to do for the safe us of essential oils with children include:

- Always make sure bottles are tightly closed and out of children's reach. Do not leave dropper dispensers in the bottles.

- Never use undiluted essential oils on children. In addition, you want to dilute them even more for kids. If you normally dilute to 2%, then for children, you would want to dilute to 1%.

- Never leave a child alone if you are using essential oils in steam inhalation. You need to ensure they are supervised at all times and that they only inhale the steam for one minute.

If you take these steps and only use the safe essential oils with children, then they can be very helpful and therapeutic for little ones.

Other Essential Oil Concerns

Depending on your situation, there are certain essential oil concerns that you need to know about. You do have to be careful of what oils you use and what they will do.

Abortifacients

- Mugwort
- Parsley Seed
- Rue
- Sage
- Sassafras

- Savin
- Tansy
- Thuja
- Wormwood
- Pennyroyal

These oils were used in folk methods for causing an abortion. Do not use them while you are pregnant and do not try to force your own abortion. They are very toxic to you as well.

Carcinogenic

Some essential oils are carcinogenic and carcinogens have been linked to cancer. These oils include:

- Calamus

- Sassafras

- Basil (if not properly used)

Basil is not necessarily dangerous, but you should only choose the oil with the highest quality to avoid the carcinogens.

Liver Toxicity

- Aniseed

- Basil

- Bay

- Buchu

- Cinnamon

- Clove

- Fennel

- Tarragon

- Cassia

These oils are not dangerous when used for external purposes. However, if you swallow them, they can be very toxic to the liver.

So, we have covered the vast majority of information you need to make smart choices for your own essential oil use. You can further your research by reading online and consulting an experienced aromatherapist. All-in-all, when essential oils are used properly, they are safe and extremely helpful. When they are not used properly, they can be very dangerous. It is your responsibility to always follow the directions. If you don't, then it is your own choice to take risks with your health.

This is an extremely important thing that you need to understand before you use essential oils in any way.

Now that you know more about essential oils, let's move on to the next section of this book.

Safety Cheat Sheet

After reading all of that safety information, you may feel a little overwhelmed by what you need to remember and what you do not. So, here is a safety cheat sheet with all of the basic information that you need to remember anytime you use essential oils.

- Always follow the directions. (Did you know that undiluted eucalyptus can be deadly?) Don't try to veer from directions or you could make a mistake.

- Always dilute properly. In the last section of this book, you will find a chart for diluting essential oils.

- Carrier oils have a limited shelf life. Keep that in mind when making a batch.

- Don't always use topical applications unless advised to. Not all oils are safe topically.

- Be very cautious when using essential oils while pregnant. Certain oils are always a pregnancy no-no.

- Children are more vulnerable to strong essential oils. Always dilute extensively before using on children.

- Always keep concentrated oils out of the reach of children.

- Only use internal essential oils on a daily basis if recommended by a doctor or other professional. Some essential oils when taken internally for a long time can result in liver failure, ulcer, and even cancer.

- Only ingest essential oils that have been deemed as safe for ingestion.

- Just because an essential oil has the name of an herb you have heard of doesn't mean it is safe.

- Just because a brand has a term like pure or high grade on the bottle doesn't necessarily make this true.

- Even if a bottle says "nutrition data" on it, this doesn't necessarily mean they are safe for ingestion.

Safety is a must when using essential oils and this fact sheet can be very helpful.

Chapter 8:

Marketing vs. Science

In the final part of this book, we will discuss helpful information, like what types of ailments can be treated with essential oils, oils that are safe and those that are toxic, recipes, and much more. However, before we get that far, we need to discuss one more topic: marketing vs. science.

What Is Marketing?

Just what is marketing? According to Forbes, "Marketing is what you say and how you say it when you want to explain how awesome your product is and why people should buy it. Marketing is an ad. Marketing is a brochure. Marketing is a Facebook page or a Twitter account. Marketing, to many business people, is simply selling at a large scale." (Brenner, 2012)

So, think about it this way: when you market, you are telling other people why they should do business with you. That's true for every company out there. Telling customers what to do means having to be as influential enough to pique the interest of potential clients.

Marketing can use many different outlets to try and get attention for the business.

There is an old concept that applies to writing and it can help you understand marketing and science here. The concept says "show don't tell." In other words, the writer shouldn't just tell the reader what is going on. They should use words to show the reader.

Now, when applying this to marketing and science, marketing is telling. You tell people they should buy from you. Science, on the other hand, is showing.

What Is Science?

According to Science Made Simple,

> "The word science comes from the Latin 'scientia,' meaning knowledge. How do we define science? According to Webster's Collegiate Dictionary, the definition of science is 'knowledge attained through study or practice,' or 'knowledge covering general truths of the operation of general laws, esp. as obtained and tested through scientific method [and] concerned with the physical world.'" (Science Definition)

Are you starting to see how that plays into the "show don't tell idea?" By using science, it is possible to actually show people how one product is better than another.

Science and Marketing

Now, we have talked about science vs. marketing and how the two are very different. Let's talk about science and marketing working together though. Look at two different scenarios:

Scenario A: A company sells essential oils. They do no research or scientific studies to back their products. Instead, they advertise and spend all of their money on marketing. They constantly tell people "hey look at our products. They are great. You should buy them." They do ok with this method, but because essential oils are just making headway in the modern market, people are leery to buy.

Scenario B: A company sells essential oils. They spend extensive time doing scientific research into the power of essential oils. Additionally, they show scientific evidence that their products are of high quality, very pure, and certified. Then, when they create marketing plans, they use this science to back up the information they provide. So, instead of saying "Buy our products because we said so," they are able to say "you should consider buying our products because we have evidence that shows they actually work."

As you can see, science and marketing are different, but they can work together to provide a solid reason why customers should buy from a certain company.

Part II: Helpful Information

Chapter 9:

Full List of Ailments to Treat Through Essential Oils

We have talked a little about the different ailments that essential oils can treat. Now, let's go into further detail. Keep in mind if you have any of these conditions, you should seek the advice of a professional doctor. However, you can enjoy relief from your symptoms from essential oils as well.

Ailment	Helpful Oil	Ailment	Helpful Oil
Abdominal Pain	Chamomile, Clove, Peppermint	Fever	Primrose, Eucalyptus, Lavender,

			Peppermint, Black Pepper, Tea Tree, Rosemary
Acne	Tea Tree, Lavender	Flu	Tea Tree, Lavender, Lemon
Addictions	Chamomile, Clary Sage, Bergamot, Jasmine, Lavender, Ylang Ylang	Gingivitis	Thyme, Eucalyptus, Chamomile, Peppermint
Athlete's Foot	Chamomile, Clove, Peppermint	Halitosis	Lavender
Bad Breath	Lavender	Hay Fever	Eucalyptus, Niaouli, Tea Tree
Bed Sores	Wheat Germ, Evening Primrose, Geranium, Tea Tree, Frankincense	Headaches	Lavender, Peppermint, Bergamot, Jojoba
Bleeding Gums	Thyme, Eucalyptus, Chamomile, Peppermint	Heartburn	Eucalyptus, Peppermint, Fennel, Grape Seed
Blisters	Lavender, Tea Tree, Chamomile	Hiccups	Chamomile

Breathing Problems	Nutmeg, Cinnamon, Eucalyptus, Ginger, Rosemary	High Blood Pressure	Hyssop, Rosemary, Sage, Thyme
Bronchitis	Basil, Benzoin, Clove, Frankincense, Pine, Tea Tree	Insect Bites	Lemongrass, Thyme, Lavender, Peppermint, Citronella
Bruises	Grape Seed, Calendula, Cypress, Fenel	Insomnia	Lavender, Neroli, Sandalwood, Clary Sage, Sandalwood
Burns	Lavender	Jetlag	Peppermint, Rosemary, Bergamot, Neroli, Geranium
Chapped Lips	Aloe Vera, Chamomile, Geranium, Neroli, Rose	Laryngitis	Geranium, Black Pepper, Tea Tree, Rosemary
Circulation Problems	Cypress, Neroli, Lemon, Geranium	Leg Cramps	Evening Primrose, Geranium
Cold Sores	Geranium, Tea Tree, Chamomile,	Mouth Ulcers	Peppermint, Thyme, Lemon, Tea Tree,

	Calendula		Geranium
Colds	Cinnamon, Cloves, Eucalyptus, Niaouli, Pine	Nausea	Mint, Fennel, Anise
Conjunctivitis	Chamomile, Witch Hazel	Nosebleed	Lemon, Lavender
Constipation	Rosemary, Lemon, Peppermint, Jojoba	Pneumonia	Pine, Cypress
Coughs	Eucalyptus, Lemon, Honey	Shock	Lemon, Geranium, Lavender, Chamomile
Cuts	Lavender, Tea Tree	Sinusitis	Rosemary, Peppermint, Thyme, Eucalyptus
Diarrhea	Peppermint, Lavender, Chamomile, Eucalyptus, Geranium	Sore Throat	Chamomile, Thyme, Lemon, Tea Tree
Diverticulosis	Peppermint, Chamomile, Rosemary, Clove	Sty	Chamomile, Rosewater

Ear Infections	Clove, Grape Seed	Swollen Ankles	Fennel, Cypress, Evening Primrose
Fainting	Peppermint, Lavender, Rosemary	Varicose Veins	Almond, Lavender, Cypress
Toothache	Clove, Chamomile, Lemon	Wounds	Lavender, Tea Tree

Some of these combinations are used for inhalation therapy, tea therapy, and topical treatments. Do not try to make your own essential oil treatment without knowing the proper recipe. Additionally, do not try to treat any serious condition without getting the direction of a physician or doctor.

Chapter 10:

List of Toxic Essential Oils

Some essential oils are toxic and they can be very, very harmful if you try to use them. We already mentioned the list of oils that are not sold in the United States. Now, let's outline very clearly the ones that are toxic. Do not ever use these for your wellbeing. They are dangerous. Here, you will find two different lists. One is a basic list of essential oils you need to avoid. The second is the list of banned essential oils according to the International Fragrance Association (IFRA).

Bitter Almond

While it's hard to imagine almond being dangerous, this essential oil most certainly is. It contains cyanide, which is a lethal poisoning. While the cyanide (prussic acid) is removed, that doesn't mean traces of it do not remain.

Boldo

Boldo leaves can be safely used in certain types of medicines, but the essential oil from this plant has been directly associated with causing convulsions.

Calamus

This is another case of a safe plant but a dangerous essential oil. The plant root itself has proven to be helpful when treating vertigo, headaches, and other problems. The essential oil, however, includes a carcinogen, which can lead to cancer. Additionally, if calamus is ingested, this can cause kidney and liver damage.

Camphor

Camphor can be used in certain external applications, but it is extremely toxic if it is ingested. In fact, it can be fatal.

Cassia

This is a good example of an essential oil that is safe for ingestion in certain treatments, but can be very dangerous topically. On the skin, it can cause extreme sensitivities and it can damage mucous membranes.

Horseradish

This herb, which can help with coughs, is too toxic to use for this type of use. It can be very irritating to eyes, skin, and mucous membranes.

Mugwort

The oil from this plant is a powerful neurotoxin, which means it can be very dangerous to your nervous system.

Mustard

The mustard seed itself is not toxic, but goes through a reaction process when it is mixed with water. For that reason, the essential oil can cause skin and mucous membrane damage.

Pennroyal

You absolutely should avoid the essential oil from this plant, even though the plant itself is very helpful for treating various conditions. The essential oil can cause acute liver and kidney damage.

Rue

Rue has a long list of toxicities, including: mucous membrane irritant, sun sensitivity, neurotoxins, and skin burning capabilities. Rue as a plant can be used in a variety of herbal medicines, but the essential oil is too dangerous for use.

Sassafras

This herb and its essential oils have been banned by the FDA. That's because it has carcinogenic qualities. Even in a very small amount, Sassafras can be lethal.

Savin

Savin is a skin irritant and an abortifacient. It contains sabinene, sabinol, and sabinyl acetate. Any oils that contain these ingredients should be avoided.

Tansy

Tansy oil can cause a variety of very scary symptoms, including organ failure, respiratory arrest, uterine bleeding, vomiting, and convulsions. It can be lethal and should be avoided.

Thuja

Thuja can be helpful as an herbal infusion, but as an essential oil, it is toxic. It can be a neurotoxin as well as an abortifacient.

Wintergreen

Wintergreen doesn't seem like it could be dangerous, and some of its ingredients can help with rheumatism and other ailments. However, if the oil is not seriously diluted, it can cause aspirin sensitivity, skin irritation, and more. The plant itself is poisonous.

Wormseed

This essential oil can be toxic to the liver and kidneys as well as damage to the heart. It is actually capable of diminishing your heart's ability to work.

Wormwood

Wormwood is actually one of the main ingredients of the alcoholic beverage, absinthe. When consumed regularly, Wormwood can cause addiction, hallucinations, convulsions, and neural side effects.

All of these essential oils are toxic and you should not use them. For the most part, they are not available in the United States, so you don't have to worry about actually purchasing them.

Essential Oils Banned by IFRA

The essential oils listed below are banned by the International Fragrance Association because they can be very dangerous. Here is a full list as well as an explanation of why the oils are dangerous.

Essential Oil	Other Names	Damage
Cade Oil	Prickly Juniper, Juniper Tar	Carcinogen (Cancer Causing)
Calamus	Sweet Flag, Myrtle, Sweet Rush, Sweet Sedge	Carcinogen
Costus Root	Kuth	Skin Sensitivity
Elecampane Oil	Scabwort	Skin Sensitivity
Fig Leaf		Skin Sensitivity
Horseradish		Overall Toxicity
Mustard	Black Mustard	Overall Toxicity
Peru Balsam	Balsamo	Skin Sensitivity
Savin Oil		Skin Sensitivity
Verbena		Skin Sensitivity
Tea Absolute		Skin Sensitivity
Sassafras		Carcinogen

Stryax Gum	Oriental Sweet Gum	Skin Sensitivity
Wormseed	Mexican Tea, Epazote	Overall Toxicity
Wormwood		Neurotoxin

In addition to the banned oils list from IFRA, they also have something called a restricted oil list. For the most part, these oils will not cause organ damage, but they can cause minor problems such as skin sensitivity. They include:

Essential Oil	Other Names	Damage
Angelica Root		Phototoxic
Bergamot	Bergamot Orange	Phototoxic
Bitter Orange	Seville Orange	Phototoxic
Cassia	Cassia Bark, Chinese Cinnamon	Sensitizer
Cinnamon Bark	Ceylon	Sensitizer
Cumin	Comino, Jeera	Phototoxic
Lemon		Phototoxic
Lime		Phototoxic
Tagetes	Muster John Henry, Khaki Weed, Stinking Rodger	Phototoxic

Oak Moss		Sensitizer
Pinaceae		Sensitizer
Rue	Herb of Grace, Herbygrass	Sensitizer
Verbena Absolute		Sensitizer
Tree Moss		Sensitizer

As you can see from this list, there are quite a few oils that are used regularly and that is because when used properly, they can be perfectly safe. That's why anytime you use essential oils of any type, you must ensure that you are using them according to directions and according to the experience of a licensed aromatherapist.

Chapter 11:

How to Dilute Essential Oils

Dilution is important as we mentioned when talking about the risks of essential oils. You should never use them at full strength, especially topically. If you do, then you could risk skin damage and other side effects. However, sometimes, it can feel difficult to find out how to dilute the oils. This chapter will cover those bases for you and help you make the right choices when mixing your ingredients.

The number one rule to remember is that essential oils should not be used "as is". They are concentrated. They have to be diluted. To dilute the oils, you will use something called carrier oil. We listed those later in the book. They can be different oils and they simply help to keep the essential oil from being too strong. Carrier oils don't really do anything other than make essential oils safe for your use.

There are different dilution levels you should use depending on who the finished product is for. We will break it down into several categories ranging from .25% all the way to 25%.

.25% Dilution

Your lowest level of essential oils will usually be 0.25%. That means you will use 1 drop of essential oil for every four tablespoons of carrier oils that you use. This is the dilution you should use for children. Remember to only use essential oils with children under the age of six with extreme caution and under the guidance of an aromatherapist or physician. Even diluted to this strength, oils can be dangerous for little ones.

1% Dilution

Another very low dilution is 1%, which equals one drop of essential oil per teaspoon of carrier oil. Or, you can figure 5-6 drops of essential oils per ounce of carrier oil. This is the best dilution for older children, pregnant women, and people with sensitive skin. Additionally, anyone with serious health conditions such as an autoimmune disorder should use this dilution.

Finally, if you plan on using the mixture as a massage oil to be applied to large areas of the body, then this is the right dilution to choose.

2% Dilution

A 2% dilution will equal about 2 drops of essential oil per teaspoon of carrier oil. On a larger level, that's 10-12 drops of oil per ounce of carrier oils. This is the ideal dilution for almost any situation and it should be safe for healthy adults.

If you plan on making skincare products that you will use on a daily basis, this is the dilution to use as well.

3% Dilution

This percentage of dilution equals about 3 drops of essential oil per teaspoon of carrier oil. Again, on a larger scale, that equals about 15-18 drops of essential oil per ounce of carrier oil.

If you have short-term health issues that need to be addressed, this is the right dilution. For example, you can use it when you are creating a blend for muscle injuries or soreness, cold congestion, and other short-term issues. If you are a healthy adult, then you can go up to 10% dilution for this purpose.

25% Dilution

This highest concentration equals about 25 drops of essential oils per teaspoon of carrier oils. If you are making the blend on a larger scale, you can use 125-150 drops of essential oil per ounce of carrier oil. This type of dilution strength should only be used on occasion. For example, if you have a sudden, painful muscle cramp in your leg, it could be useful, or the right blend may help severe bruising heal.

Neat

Using essential oils neat refers to using them without any type of dilution. You should do this with extreme caution because most essential oils will be too strong. The only essential oil that is totally safe in a neat form is lavender. It can be used to treat bug bites, small scratches, burns, and other skin irritations without any dilution.

Converting Essential Oil Drops

Sometimes, when you are using essential oils for various recipes, they may give you an amount to use other than drops. This can make it difficult for you to do conversions. Below are helpful conversion charts that will make your life easier when you are mixing recipes of any type.

Drops	Teaspoons	Milliliters	Ounces
100	1	5	1/6
200	2	10	1/3
300	3	15	½
400	4	20	2/3
500	5	25	5/6
600	6	30	1

Additionally, every drop of essential oils equals about 30 mg and 900 mg equals one ml.

What Carriers Should I Use?

So, you have a list of carrier oils earlier in this book. You know how to dilute your essential oils. Likely, your next question would be which carrier oils should you use in which dilution. That can be confusing, so here are some quick tips to help you.

If you are making a lotion, you want something that will absorb quickly and actually get into the skin before it evaporates. You should look for a lotion base that includes shea butters and beeswax. Avoid carrier lotions that contain high amounts of water since the water will evaporate before the lotion is absorbed.

If you are using carrier oils, here are some quick tips on when to use each type. Carrier oils are great for all sorts of products from home cleaners to toners and shampoo.

- With jojoba oil, you can use it to dilute almost any essential oil. It has a very light fragrance and its chemical makeup is very close to your skin's own oil. It also has a long shelf-life (up to a year) meaning you don't have to worry about it going bad quickly.

- With Avocado oil, you can expect a mild aroma and plenty of hydration for the skin. It is very good for helping fight the effects of inflammation and scarring too.

- Coconut oil is usually in a firm solid form, but if you purchase fractioned coconut oil, it is already in a liquid state. This is the perfect option for almost anything because it is good for hair and skin. If you wish to create a blend for someone with sensitive or acne prone skin, this is a good choice.

- Tamanu Oil can be used if you are creating a burn blend because it is both germicidal and analgesic. Additionally, you can use it for scar treating formulas.

Butters are especially useful if you want to absorb the essential oils slowly. That makes them good for deep moisturizing treatments, conditioners, and other bath and body products.

- Shea butter is the most commonly used. It makes a good choices for deep moisturizers, foot treatments, lip balms and deodorants.

- Cocoa butter is a very pleasant smelling carrier and it repels water so that your skin almost has a seal on it. it is very good for treating fine lines and wrinkles on the face.

- Kombo butter has a very oily, sticky consistency so it is only good in certain situations. If you are making a mixture to fight joint inflammation or to treat fungal infections on the feet, this is a good choice.

Staying Safe with Carrier Oils

Just as we discussed with essential oils, you need to make sure you are safe in your use of carrier oils. Here are a few tips to keep in mind:

- Carriers usually have a shelf life of 6 to 12 months.

- Canola, soy, and other vegetable oils are not good as carriers. They are not healthy and will clog the pores.

- If a carrier oil is cloudy or has a strange odor, it's time to throw it out.

- Don't purchase carrier oils that are processed or refined.

You will have very little luck using water as a carrier because it doesn't mix with essential oils. If you are making a cleaning spray that includes water, you will need to shake thoroughly before each use to ensure the water and essential oils have mixed together.

Chapter 12:

Using Essential Oils in Recipes: Bath and Body

Now that you have read this book and you know everything you need to about essential oils, let's get started looking at some recipes that use the oils for all sorts of different products for your health as well as for household cleaning and other chores. Remember that you can get more information on different ways to use essential oils in recipes from an aromatherapist as well.

Shampoo

When using essential oils in shampoo, make sure you are diluting them enough so that they do not cause eye irritation. Here is a good recipe that includes the use of a shampoo base, which you can find from natural product sellers.

7 ounces of shampoo base (make sure it is unscented, SLS free, and natural)

40 drops of Lavender oil

10 drops of Rosemary oil

All that you need to do is blend these ingredients together thoroughly and store in a convenient bottle. If you want to make sure your hair is hydrated, consider adding jojoba to the ingredients as well.

This next shampoo recipe requires that you make your own base, but the process is not that difficult.

8 ounces of distilled water (it must be distilled or you will end up with buildup)

3 ounces of liquid castile soap

3 tablespoons of aloe vera gel

One quarter teaspoon of jojoba oil

30 drops of rosemary oil

All that you have to do is mix these ingredients together thoroughly. Here are some variations you can make to this recipe depending on your hair type:

- Add chamomile and calendula if you have blond hair

- Add nettle and sage if you have dark hair

- Add violet leaf and extra jojoba if you have dry hair

- If you have brittle hair, add nettle

- Add tea tree oil if you have dandruff

- If you have extremely dry hair, add olive oil, sesame oil, or almond oil (note this can make your hair feel greasy unless it is extremely dry)

Essential oil shampoo is easy to make and can be very useful. Before you use a shampoo involving essential oils, however, do a skin patch test on your wrist to make sure you will not have any reactions. Never use any oils that are skin irritants in your shampoos.

Facial Scrubs

Facial scrubs can help to slough away dead skin and make sure your face is glowing and healthy. You can use essential oils as long as you stick with the ones that will not cause skin or mucous membrane irritation.

A very simple oat facial scrub includes the following ingredients:

> 3 tablespoons of raw oats
>
> Honey
>
> ¼ tablespoon of apple cider vinegar
>
> 1 drop of basil essential oil

The first thing you will need to do is crush the oats so that they become smaller and easier to mix. Then, add in your other ingredients until smooth. If you have problems with your skin, like acne or redness, you can add in tea tree oil as well.

The mixture will be sticky and you can rub it into your face with circular motions. Do not allow it near the eyes and mouth. Allow the scrub to stay on your face for about 10 to 15 minutes and then wash thoroughly.

Another great ingredient you can use for your facial scrubs is brown sugar. The sugar will do very well with sloughing away dead skin and different ingredients and oils can be added. Here are some ideas:

- Combine a cup of brown sugar, a half cup of coconut oil, and a drop of lavender. This will create a basic scrub that can be used on your face or body.

- Mix a cup of sugar, a half cup of almond oil, 15 drops of lavender, and ½ teaspoon of vanilla extract. You will get a sugary, relaxing facial scrub that will help you destress.

- Mix ¼ cup of sugar, a half cup of coconut oil, and several drops of either lemon or orange essential oils. This refreshing scrub will help wake you up in the morning.

The nice things about facial scrubs is that they are very easy to make and aside from the essential oils, only need common household ingredients you likely already have in your kitchen cabinet.

Creams and Lotions

Aromatherapy is especially useful in creams and lotions. After all, why should you just use a fake scent when you could use natural, essential oils that will actually help your mood or health at the same time? To make these lotions, you will need to start with a base and then you can add various essential oils as needed. The base includes:

One half cup of olive oil

¼ cup of coconut oil

¼ cup of beeswax

One teaspoon of vitamin E

2 tablespoons of Shea butter

Mix all of the ingredients in a heat safe jar – a mason jar is perfect – and then fill a saucepan with water and place on medium heat. Loosely put the lid on the jar and then set it directly into the pan of warming water. Stir ingredients within the jar occasionally. Once everything is completely melted, you have your lotion base. Now, you can add essential oils. Here are some suggestions:

- Add peppermint for a refreshing lotion to keep in the kitchen or to use in winter

- Add peppermint, wintergreen, and ginger if you want a refreshing lotion that will soothe sore muscles

- If you want to create a facial lotion, then add coconut or calendula oil

- For a soothing and stress-relieving cream, add lavender and vanilla

- For a skin soothing lotion, add green tea and peppermint

- If you want a lotion to use on babies and children, then seriously dilute chamomile and include in the lotion (avoid using essential oils on infants unless you have consulted an aromatherapist and your pediatrician).

If you don't want to go through the process of making lotion from scratch, you can still create essential oil creams. This aromatherapy lotion is a perfect combination of essential oils for a great scent, relaxation, and good skin.

You will need 8 ounces of unscented body lotion. Look for types that are all-natural, SLS free and unscented. You can find these at all-natural stores.

10 drops of patchouli

5 drops of carrot seed

10 drops of sandalwood

These essential oils will add a lovely scent while aiding in easing dry skin. You may wish to lower the amount of each essential oil if the scent is too harsh. This lotion can be used on the hands or body, but should not be used on the face.

A body butter is like a lotion, but it is much thicker and is very good for treating severely dry skin. The easiest way to make essential oil body butter is to use coconut oil. You don't need any other base. Here are two recipes for coconut body butter that you could choose.

One cup of coconut oil

10 drops of Eucalyptus

10 drops of lavender

10 drops of tea tree oil

All you need to do is mix these ingredients together and you will have a luxurious cream to use on the driest skin you may have. Another recipe for coconut body butter includes:

One cup of coconut oil

1 tablespoon of extra virgin olive oil

5 drops of eucalyptus

5 drops of peppermint oil

These are not the only ways you can use essential oils for your body. Let's look next at hair treatments.

Hair Treatment

This first recipe is one designed to soften and strengthen hair. It will also help to promote hair growth.

2 drops of Thyme

3 drops of rosemary

2 drops of cedar

1 tablespoon of jojoba

Mix these ingredients thoroughly and then massage the mixture in the scalp. Rinse with cool water before shampooing hair. You can use this every night if you have normal to dry hair. If you have oily hair, you may want to limit use to two to three times a week.

Dry shampoo is especially useful for keeping your hair fresh between shampooing. It's not good to wash your hair every single day, but you don't want to deal with oily, flat hair either. That's when you can use dry shampoo. Here is a great essential oil recipe to use:

25 grams of purified talc (available at any pharmacy)

4 drops of rosemary

4 drops of tea tree oil

4 drops of lavender

Place the talc in a blender and then slowly add the oils, one drop at a time while keeping the blender on a low speed. Brush just a teaspoon or two of the talc into your hair whenever needed. Make sure you don't allow the dry shampoo to clump.

This next recipe is for a scalp stimulating lotion. It will help give your scalp a boost and that means you will be able to enjoy healthier hair.

10 mL of alcohol (you can use vodka as long as it is not flavored)

30 mL of distilled water

5 drops of rosemary oil

5 drops of chamomile

5 drops of lavender

Once you have everything mixed together, you can simply massage it into your scalp and then rinse before shampooing.

Finally, let's look at a recipe for a shine rinse. This will be used after your shampooing as a final rinse to make sure your hair is shiny and full of life.

4 teaspoons of distilled water

2 tablespoons of apple cider vinegar

3 drops of lemon

After you have shampooed and conditioned your hair, simply rinse with this mixture. You don't even have to rinse out either.

Perfume

If you would like to make your own perfumes, then you must understand how the essential oils are grouped. They split into nine different categories and they don't all necessarily mix well together for perfumes. So, here are the nine categories and samples of the oils that fit into them.

Category	Sample Oils
Floral	Lavender, Neroli, Jasmine
Woodsy	Pine, Cedar
Earthy	Oakmoss, Patchouli, Vetiver
Herbaceous	Marjoram, Basil, Rosemary
Minty	Spearmint, Peppermint
Medicinal	Eucalyptus, Tea Tree, Cajuput
Spicy	Cinnamon, Clove, Nutmeg
Oriental	Patchouli, Ginger
Citrus	Lemon, Lime, Orange

The first rule to remember is that any oils that fit within the same category will mix well together. Certain categories do blend well with each other as well. For example:

- You can mix floral scents with woodsy, citrus, or spicy scents.

- You can mix woodsy oils with scents from any other category.

- Spicy and oriental scents work well with floral and citrus.

- Minty scents will work well with herbaceous, earthy, woodsy, or citrus oils.

You have to know how to blend oils properly to get a lovely perfume smell. One mistake and you could end up either wasting a lot of oils or not getting the results you wanted. The first thing you need to understand is top, middle and base notes.

Top notes are those that you smell within one or two hours of using the perfume.

Middle notes are those that appear when the top notes have evaporated, showing up between two and four hours of use.

Base notes are those that appear when everything else has evaporated and they last the longest time.

Now, to get the most out of your perfume, you need to blend the right top, middle, and base notes. It can come along with a little trial and error, but it's best to start with a very small amount of drops until you find the right blend. The best way to find your perfect perfume is to follow these tips from AromaWeb.

- Start with just the essential oils themselves. After you have found the perfect scent, you can use carrier oils or alcohol to finish the blend. This way, you will waste as little as possible.

- Keep a notebook that you use for information about different numbers of drops you use. If you are trying different things, you may forget what you did and that means you will have to start the trial and error process all over again.

- Follow these percentages: 30% top notes, 50% middle notes, and 20% base notes.

- Don't immediately start making the perfume in bulk as soon as you find a scent combination you like. Let it sit for a few days to see if you still love the smell. (Aromatic Blending of Essential Oils)

You will need a cologne or perfume base to go along with your oil blends, so here are four different carrier bases you can create:

Carrier 1: Oil Perfume

15 to 25 drops of the perfume blend you decide on.

1 tablespoon of jojoba oil (you could also use sweet almond)

Blend everything together and store it in an airtight container. Try using a dark container so that the blend will not be changed by the light. Additionally, this is a strong essential oil base. For that reason, you need to do a skin patch test on the inside of your wrist to make sure you don't have any reactions before you use the perfume regularly.

Carrier 2: Alcohol Base Perfume

With this recipe, you are going to use vodka. Just make sure you choose a very high quality version of the alcohol.

4.25 teaspoons of Vodka

1.5 teaspoons of distilled water

60 drops of your chosen perfume blend

You will need to store this perfume in an airtight, dark container and you need to shake it a couple of times a day for two weeks to make sure the ingredients blend well. Then, after two weeks, run the perfume through a coffee filter and then replace in the bottle for use. This is also a higher concentration oil, so you need to make sure you test it on the inside of one wrist before use.

Carrier 3: Cologne

If you are planning to make a more masculine cologne, then use this recipe.

4.5 teaspoons of Vodka

2 teaspoons of distilled water

30 drops of your essential oil blend

You will need to follow the same steps as carrier two in order to ensure the ingredients mix well together. This carrier works well with a fine mist spray bottle too.

Carrier 4: Body Splash

If you want something light, airy and useful for a refreshing scent throughout the day, this is a good option.

4.5 teaspoons of Vodka

2 teaspoons of distilled water

18 drops of your essential oil blend

Make sure to follow the steps listed above for shaking the scent regularly and then filtering it through a coffee filter. Then, you can use it in a fine mist spray bottle.

All of these recipes will offer great scents for your bath and body needs. You can enjoy refreshing scents, clean hair, and a smooth face. The best part is you will also get to enjoy the aromatherapy benefits of these oils. Just make sure you always do skin patch tests when you make these recipes to ensure you will not have a reaction to the oils. A skin patch test can easily be done on the inside of one wrist. Just dab the recipe on and then wait several hours to see if you have any reaction.

After that, you can mix up larger quantities of these different recipes so that you always have them available when needed.

Chapter 13:

Using Essential Oils in Recipes: Household Cleaners

There are also numerous different ways you can use essential oils when you clean your home. These recipes will offer cleaning power, natural disinfecting, and a wonderful scent that will linger in your home for days. To make these recipes, you will need to gather a few ingredients. Most are available in your grocery store:

- Baking Soda

- Essential Oils

- Citrus Seed Extract (Available online and through all-natural stores)

- Lemon Juice

- Liquid Castile Soap (Available at health food stores)

- Kosher Salt

- Vinegar

- Washing Soda (usually available on the laundry products aisle)

Once you have these ingredients, you will be ready to start making your own household cleaners.

Disinfectant

This is one of the easiest essential oil blends that you could make and it is very useful because it can be employed to disinfect almost anything. All you need is three ingredients and a spray bottle:

2 cups hot water

10 drops of Thyme or Lemon

¼ cup washing soda

Mix everything together in a spray bottle. Spray surfaces to disinfect and then wipe clean with a sponge or cloth.

Dishwashing Soap

Let's look at two recipes for dishwashing soap. The first is a liquid blend you can use when you are washing dishes by hand. The second is a powder you can use in your dishwasher.

Liquid Blend:

> 20 drops of lime or lemon essential oil
>
> 10 drops of sweet orange
>
> 5 drops of citrus seed extract
>
> Liquid castile soap

Use a spray bottle that holds about 22 ounces and add in the castile soap. Then add in the essential oils and shake well.

Powder Blend:

You can make this recipe in bulk because it stays very well and can be kept for whenever you need it.

> 3 cups washing soda
>
> 1 cup baking soda
>
> 5 drops of citrus essential oil (added slowly with powders in blender)

With this, just make the ingredients and then store in a box.

Sink Cleaner

If you want to make a scrubber to keep your sinks clean, then you only need the following ingredients:

¼ cup of washing soda

½ cup of baking soda

8 drops of tea tree oil (or rosemary)

¾ cup of vinegar

Blend all ingredients together except for the vinegar. Then, sprinkle the powder onto the sink and use a sponge to scrub away stains. Finally, rinse the sink with vinegar. You can rinse again with hot water to get rid of the vinegar smell if you would like.

Oven Cleaner

Ovens are so hard to keep clean, but this recipe can come in handy. You will need to mix up the ingredients and then scrub the oven with fine steel wool. The ingredients needed include:

½ cup salt (more for an especially dirty oven)
¼ cup of washing soda
1 box of baking soda
10 drops of Thyme
10 drops of Lemon
¼ cup water
¾ cup vinegar

Blend the salt and two sodas together along with water and you will have a thick paste. Preheat the oven at about 250 degrees and then spread the paste on the on the walls of the oven. Allow this to sit for about half an hour. Then, mix vinegar with the essential oils in a spray bottle, spray over the paste and wipe the oven clean.

Toilet Cleaner

If you want to get your toilet clean, then you will enjoy this mix. You can use it for the bowl of the toilet as well as the seat and underneath the seat. It doesn't just clean, it also disinfects for a germ-free bathroom.

2 cups of water

½ cup liquid castile soap

1 tablespoon of tea tree oil

10 drops peppermint

Mix everything together in a spray bottle and then use it to clean all surfaces of the toilet.

Carpet Shampoo

When you clean carpets, you obviously don't want to put anything on them that could be dangerous for your skin, for children, or for pets. This shampoo will do the trick.

3 cups of water

1 cup of liquid castile soap

10 drops peppermint

Mix everything well and then hand rub it into soiled areas of the carpet. Allow this to sit before sponging off the ingredients and vacuuming when dry.

Pest Control

Tired of ants in the kitchen or cockroaches getting into the house? Here are some essential oil mixes you can use. For these recipes, you will need the following ingredients:

- Diatomaceous Earth

- Apple Cider Vinegar

- Essential Oils You Choose (see chart below)

- Lemon Juice

- Peroxide

- Salt

- Baking Soda

When you use these recipes, you can expect results, and the best part is you don't have to deal with that noxious bug spray scent in the meantime. To determine the right essential oils to get rid of those pests, here is a chart of what will work with which bug:

Essential Oil	Pest Power
Peppermint, Eucalyptus	Spiders, ants, cockroaches, fleas, ticks, beetles, gnats, lice, silverfish, moths
Cedar Wood	Lice, moths, slugs, snails

Lemongrass	Fleas, ticks, flies, lice, silverfish, mosquitoes, moths
Lavender	Fleas, ticks, mosquitos, biting flies
Sage, Oregano, Thyme	Beetles, flies
Lemon, Lime, Orange	Fleas, ants, cockroaches, biting flies

To create a pest control spray, mix 20 drops of peppermint oil along with water. Shake well in a spray bottle and then you can spray on plants, on the walls, and on the floors.

To kill flies and gnats, mix together 16 ounces of alcohol, 1 teaspoon of eucalyptus, 1 teaspoon of peppermint, and 1 teaspoon of castile soap. Add all of this to a spray bottle and then fill the rest of the way with water and mix well. This will help kill the bugs and will repel them as well.

A bug repellant can be made with apple cider vinegar, water, and lemon essential oils. Then, spray it in the corners of the room as well as in windows and across bottoms of the door frame. This will keep bugs from ever coming into your house.

To repel mosquitoes, you will need:

A spray bottle

Peppermint, rosemary, citronella, or clove

Jojoba oil

Mix your blend at these numbers: ¼ ounce of essential oils and ¾ ounce of jojoba. Blend these ingredients in a spray bottle and shake thoroughly. This blend will actually work to repel mosquitoes and can be used as an antibacterial, which is great for the summer months.

This is just the beginning too. There are numerous ways you can use essential oils in your home for cleaners and to repel bugs.

Chapter 14:

Using Essential Oils in Recipes: Aromatherapy

Finally, let's discuss how you can use aromatherapy and essential oils for your emotional wellbeing. You can use these ingredients in a diffuser to ensure your home smells nice and has the right effect on your emotions considering what you are trying to accomplish.

First, we will look at the various essential oils that will help with your emotional concerns. Then, later in the chapter, we will look at some specific recipes.

Anger Management

If you are looking for essential oils that will help dispel your anger and ensure you are calm (this can be used for you or anyone in the household), then consider the following oils:

- Bergamot

- Frankincense

- Geranium

- Grapefruit

- Lemon

- Neroli

- Orange

- Rose

- Sandalwood

All of these essential oils can have a calming effect on anger and are perfect for the diffuser.

Anxiety

Anxiety or anxiety attacks can be calmed with several essential oils as well, including:

- Bergamot

- Jasmine

- Neroli

- Orange

- Patchouli

- Roman Chamomile

- Rose

- Vetiver

- Sandalwood

This can help with many types of anxiety, whether you have been diagnosed with an anxiety disorder or you just get anxious from time to time. However, this should not be a replacement for any medications you have been prescribed by the doctor. Consider the aromatherapy as a supplement for your treatment.

Confidence Building

If you have trouble with confidence or you have a big presentation or project ahead, consider these oils:

- Laurel

- Bergamot

- Cypress

- Grapefruit

- Orange

- Rosemary

Using these in the diffuser can give you a confidence boost at just the right time.

Depression

Just as mentioned with anxiety, if you have depression, then essential oils and aromatherapy are not a replacement for your medications. You need to stick with what your doctor has prescribed. However, using these oils in a diffuser can help ease the symptoms you may be experiencing or they may be helpful if you do not have clinical depression or you are dealing with a depressing event in life.

- Bergamot

- Frankinscence

- Clary Sage

- Geranium

- Jasmine

- Lavender

- Lemon

- Neroli

- Orange

- Roman Chamomile

- Rose

- Sandalwood

Using these essential oils can help to lift your mood and calm the depressive thoughts you may be having.

Fatigue

Fatigue, burnout at work, or exhaustion can ruin your day and make it very hard for you to remain productive. These essential oils can help:

- Basil

- Bergamot

- Clary Sage

- Frankincense

- Jasmine

- Lemon

- Patchouli

- Peppermint

- Rosemary

- Sandalwood

These essential oils will boost your energy levels and help you ease the effects of fatigue on your mind and body.

Fear

Fear can be paralyzing and, in most situations, it elicits a fight or flight response. That makes it very hard for you to function when fear is ruling your body and mind. There are several essential oils you can use in a few different ways to ease the effects of fear, though:

- Bergamot

- Clary Sage

- Vetiver

- Sandalwood

- Orange

- Jasmine

- Roman Chamomile

- Frankincense

There are several different ways you can use essential oils to ease the effects of fear as well. Let's discuss three of them:

- To make a blend for your diffuser, mix Clary Sage, Roman Chamomile, and Vetiver together. Add 20 drops of this blend to your diffuser.

- To make a bath oil blend, mix together sandalwood and orange. Then, add 15 drops of the blend to your bath.

- To make massage oil, use a massage oil base or recipe and then mix together Jasmine, Frankincense, and Clary Sage. Then add 10 drops to the bath oil base.

Depending on your level of fear over anything, from spiders to the future to the loss of a family member, you can use these recipes to overcome it.

Grief

If you have ever experienced grief, then you know how overwhelming it can be. Grief itself can cause anger, frustration, extreme sadness, and any emotion in between. The loss can be unbearable. However, there are essential oils that can help with this:

- Rose (the most helpful at fighting the mental strain of grief)

- Sandalwood

- Cypress

- Neroli

- Frankincense

When grief from loss is consuming you, this is an excellent way to at least take the edge off. While you cannot erase grief completely, you can make it easier to manage.

Happiness and Peace

If you want to enhance the happy, peaceful feelings in your life, then essential oils can help with this as well. The different blends that can do this include:

- Blend: Bergamot and Grapefruit

- Blend: Geranium, Orange, and Frankincense

- Blend: Sandalwood, Bergamot, and Rose

- Blend: Lemon, Grapefruit, Neroli, and Rose

These types of blends can be used in bath and body products or in a diffuser so that you can enjoy the aromatherapy benefits.

Insecurity

When you feel insecure, it is very hard to do anything. You will not be able to work confidently or even represent yourself in any situation in a confident manner. So, to boost your security and let go of things that are making you insecure, consider these essential oils:

- Bergamot

- Jasmine

- Vetiver

- Cedarwood

- Frankincense

Blends using these essential oils will help to ensure you can boost your own confidence and get over your insecurities.

Irritability

Do you ever have those days when it seems like anything that happens ticks you off? Irritability can come up for many different reasons, including changes in your body chemistry, stress, illness, extra work, and more. So, to ease the effects of irritability, consider these essential oils:

- Mandarin

- Lavender

- Neroli

- Roman Chamomile

- Sandalwood

Using these essential oil blends in a diffuser or bath oil will help ensure you feel more calm, relaxed, and less irritable about little things.

Loneliness

Whether you have moved to a new town, lost a loved one, started college, started a new job, or done anything else that has resulted in lonely feelings, the blends listed here can help extensively. The loneliness fighting essential oils include:

- Rose, Frankincense and Bergamot

- Bergamot and Clary Sage

- Bergamot and Roman Chamomile

- Frankincense and Clary Sage

You can use these blends in bath and body products as well as diffusers to ensure you feel less lonely no matter your current situation.

Memory and Concentration

There are plenty of different reasons why you may have trouble concentrating. Perhaps you haven't gotten enough sleep or maybe you have been under the weather. In any situation, when you need to improve your memory and concentration, consider these essential oils:

- Rosemary

- Lemon

- Cypress

- Peppermint

- Basil

- Hyssop

Peppermint mixed with lemon and cypress can be extremely helpful at strengthening your memory and concentration skills.

Panic

Essential oils cannot completely take away panic attacks. If you are having the physical symptoms of this type of attack, you should see a physician. Panic attacks can be all-consuming, making it hard for you to even function. Using essential oils can help you lessen the mental impact of panic, and that can, in turn, ease the chances of having a panic attack at all:

- Helichrysum

- Frankincense

- Rose

- Lavender

- Neroli

If you are just feeling panicky, using these essential oils can help. If you have regular panic attacks, using these blends regularly can help quell the symptoms and make it easier for you to live your life.

Stress Reduction

People often think that stress is "just a part of life." However, stress on a chronic level can be extremely debilitating. It can make you sick and it can affect all parts of your life. You should not have to constantly cope with stress. Essential oils and aromatherapy can be a fantastic way to ease the effects of stress, no matter the source of that stress in the first place.

Here are three different blends that can be used to ease the effects of stress on you, mentally and physically:

- Clary Sage, Lemon, and Lavender

- Bergamot, Geranium, and Frankincense

- Roman Chamomile, Lavender, and Vetiver

Of course, if you use other stress-relieving methods in conjunction with these essential oil blends, you will find it much easier to live a much more comfortable life.

Overall Emotional Well-Being

The following lists of blends can be used in order to soothe bad emotions and boost good ones on an overall basis. No matter what you may be feeling, these aromas can help you feel better. Let's look at a total of 10 different blends:

1. Jasmine, Lime, Sweet Orange, and Cinnamon

2. Patchouli, Vanilla, Linden Blossom, and Neroli

3. Lime, Bergamot, Ylang Ylang, and Rose

4. Rosewood, Lavender, and Ylang Ylang

5. Rosemary, Peppermint, Lavender, and Roman Chamomile

6. Bergamot, Lemon, and Spearmint

7. Bergamot, Lavender, and Cypress

8. Spearmint, Lavender, and Sweet Orange

9. Jasmine, Sweet Orange, and Patchouli

10. Sandalwood and Neroli

When you blend these types and include them in a diffuser or use them in bath and body products, they will ensure you feel better overall. They make great options for easing negative emotions and boosting positive ones. As a result, you will just be in a better mood, so they are excellent choices to use every day.

Finally, let's look at some miscellaneous recipes you can make with your essential oils and blends.

Chapter 15:

Using Essential Oils in Recipes: Miscellaneous

Finally, here are some recipes you can use for miscellaneous purposes. Some of them will help with bath and body in some ways while others are just handy to keep around.

Bug Bite Treatment

You know how frustrating a bug bite can be. It itches and becomes very painful. It can even get irritated and inflamed. To make an instant bug bite soother, you will need a roller bottle. Then, create a mix with the following ingredients:

- 25% tea tree oil

- 25% lavender oil

- 50% jojoba

Once you have mixed this up, you can roll it directly on the bug bite and enjoy instant relief. Additionally, it will help to keep the bug bite from becoming inflamed over time.

Varicose Vein Treatment

Varicose veins occur in the legs because circulation is cut off for one reason or another. Many people who stand on their feet all day develop this problem. While varicose veins generally do not cause you any problems, they are unattractive. This treatment can help fight the look of these veins.

- One ounce of jojoba oil

- 2 drops bergamot

- 2 drops grapefruit

- 2 drops sweet orange

- 1 drop frankincense

- 1 drop neroli

Mix all of the ingredients together in a bottle and then rub on your skin with your hands when needed. Make sure you keep the oil in a dark bottle. This is a 2% dilution, so make sure that is ok for you.

Stretch Mark Treatment

Stretch marks are extremely unsightly but they are a problem for many people. They tend to appear on the legs, belly and arms (and for women, on the breasts). They appear when someone has gone through a growth spurt, when they have lost a lot of weight, or when a woman has a baby. The stretch mark treatment will help lessen the look of these unsightly lines:

- 3 ounces of jojoba oil

- 20 drops tangerine or sweet orange

- 10 drops of frankincense

- 4 drops of neroli

- 10 drops of geranium

Mix the ingredients together in a squeeze bottle and then apply with your hands as needed.

Scar Treatment

If you have scars, then you likely would prefer to get rid of them. This treatment can help with that. You will need:

- Tamanu Oil as a carrier

- 8 drops of helichrysum

- 8 drops of frankincense

- 4 drops of geranium oil

Mix everything together and keep in a small bottle. Then, you can rub the blend on your fingers and then apply directly to the scar.

Sponge Refreshing Treatment

Sponges get pretty gross over time but you shouldn't have to automatically throw them out. Instead, you can use this essential oil blend.

- 4 ounces of vinegar

- 30 drops of peppermint oil

- 30 drops of lemon oil

- ½ ounce of castile soap

This works best in a pump bottle or one that you use for lotion. Then, whenever your sponge needs refreshing, just squirt the oil on it, wring out and rinse.

All Natural Bleach

Sometimes, you need bleach, but you may not want to use that toxic chemical form you can get in the store. Not to worry. You can make your own essential oil blend bleach that will work very well for cleaning laundry and surfaces.

- 1.5 cups of peroxide

- Half a cup of lemon juice

- 12 drops of lemon essential oil

- Water

Mix this together and you have your very own bleach that is all-natural and much nicer smelling too.

Hair Growth Serum

If you are trying to get your hair to grow out, but you haven't had much luck, then this serum can help. You only need two ingredients combined in a squeeze bottle.

- 2 ounces of castor oil as a carrier

- 12 drops of rosemary4

Mix these together in a bottle. Then, massage about half a teaspoon into your hair. If you have a thinning scalp area, then pay special attention to this area. Allow this treatment to stay on your hair for about 20-30 minutes before you shampoo.

You can use this about 2-3 times a week for best results. Do not use this serum on children under the age of 10.

Anti-Germ Blend for Children

This is a great recipe to use as a germicide with children. Because it is diluted and uses safe oils, it can be used for children even as young as six months old (again, always get the ok from a physician before using any oil blends on babies).

- 30 drops of sweet orange

- 40 drops of cinnamon leaf

- 25 drops of fir needle

You can make this mix and use it in several different ways. In a diffuser, add five drops and then leave on in the child's room. Add five drops to a small bottle and wave it under the child's nose to dispel any germs in the air.

Antibacterial Hand Spray

Kids get germs on their hands all the time. It can be very hard to keep them safe from bacteria of all types. This hand spray can take the place of the antibacterial cleansers you can get at the store (they contain alcohol and burn!).

For this spray, you will need a small spray bottle that you can keep with you. Then, mix the following together:

- 3 tablespoons of witch hazel

- 2 teaspoons of almond oil

- 3 drops of anti-germ blend described above

Mix these together and then spray on your child's hands. You can use this on even small children and babies. If you want to turn this blend into a spray for adults, then boost the dilution to .50%.

With these different ingredients and recipes, you will see that there are so many different things you can do with essential oils. You are not just limited to lotions and soaps. You can actually replace almost any household item if you know the right recipe.

Now that you have information on how to make many different things with essential oils and blends, you can move on to the last chapter where we describe how you can find out more. After all, there is so much information about essential oils out there. Whether you want to research the oils or even find books of hundreds of recipes, you will find resources in the next chapter.

Chapter 16:

Further Resources

If you want to keep learning about essential oils or you are interested in finding more recipes or other uses for these oils, there are plenty of resources available to you. You can also look on Google to find even more resources. There is so much information out there. However, if you start looking on your own, be very careful and only research with reputable sources. You can come across some disreputable or unknowledgeable sites that may recommend things that could be dangerous for you. Additionally, if you are reading anything that suggests you use banned oils, then move on.

So, let's look at some reputable resources you can use to learn about essential oils in general and the dōTERRA brand specifically.

Websites

One good resource, of course, is the dōTERRA website, which can be found at www.dōTERRA.com. You will find information about the products available as well as further resources on all of the research that dōTERRA does in order to ensure they offer high quality oils and products.

AromaWeb offers a vast dictionary of information about essential oils as well as recipes that you could try. You can find it at www.aromaweb.com

PubMed is a website that conglomerates all types of medical research studies and publications. You can find very educational material about the science of essential oils. The website is available at www.PubMed.com.

dōTERRA Specific Websites

If you would like to get involved with dōTERRA specifically, whether as an independent consultant or as a customer, these websites can help you.

- www.MydōTERRA.com/ -- A virtual back office platform that you can use as a consultant.

- www.doTERRAPro.com – This website offers training for essential oils consultants and even has community forums so that you can talk with other consultants too.

- www.doTERRATOOLS.com offers you product information for all of the dōTERRA products so that you will be able to educate yourself more.

- www.doTERRAEveryday.com gives practical news and advice about using dōTERRA products.

- www.OilsMentor.com gives you instructional and educational material about working as a consultant of dōTERRA products and essential oils.

Books

The Illustrated Encyclopedia of Essential Oils by Julia Lawless

Essential Oils for Pregnancy, Birth, and Babies by Stephanie Fritz

Essential Oils Pocket Reference by Gary Young

The Complete Book of Essential Oils and Aromatherapy by Valerie Ann Worwood

Essential Oils for Beginners by Althea Press

Essential Oils for Mental Health by Harper Evans

Surviving When Modern Medicine Fails by Gary Young

Essential Oils: 60 Oils That You Need to Use and How to Use Them Now by Leon Green

Emotional Healing and Essential Oils by Daniel Macdonald

Conclusion

Many people don't recognize just how many uses for essential oils there actually are. These oils are all-natural, and since they are extracted from plants, they allow you to accomplish a great deal without exposing yourself to chemicals.

You can use essential oils to help boost your mental state, to take care of your skin and body, and even clean your home. They are extremely versatile. However, they will only work so well if you choose high quality oils. That means working with a seller like dōTERRA, whom you can trust. This way, you can ensure the oils you purchase are harvested correctly and at the right time for the best results from these essential oils.

The final thing that you should take away from this book is that it is extremely important to follow all directions and use essential oils safely. If used in the wrong manner, they can be dangerous. People don't always understand this because they assume anything natural should be safe. However, because these oils are such a high concentration of plant matter, they can be dangerous, causing everything from minor skin irritation to greatly enhancing the risk of cancer.

If you use a dependable and safe seller like dōTERRA, though, and you follow all the instructions, you should have no problem using essential oils properly. They can certainly enhance your life, so you do not want to miss out on them. If you need assistance go to http://www.mydoterra.com/essentialoilsheal/contactUs.html

Now, go out there and explore how essential oils can help you personally.

Works Cited

Are Essential Oils Safe? (n.d.). Retrieved July 9, 2014, from University of Minnesota: http://www.takingcharge.csh.umn.edu/explore-healing-practices/aromatherapy/are-essential-oils-safe

Aromatherapy. (n.d.). Retrieved July 9, 2014, from NYU Langone Medical Center: http://www.med.nyu.edu/content?ChunkIID=37427

Aromatic Blending of Essential Oils. (n.d.). Retrieved July 11, 2014, from AromaWeb: http://www.aromaweb.com/articles/aromaticblending.asp

Brenner, M. (2012, August 9). *What Is Marketing?* Retrieved July 15, 2014, from Forbes: http://www.forbes.com/sites/sap/2012/08/09/what-is-marketing/

CPTG Certified Therepuetic Grade. (n.d.). Retrieved July 14, 2014, from Share doTERRA: http://www.sharedoterra.com/wp-content/uploads/2011/09/CPTG%20statement%20Dr.%20Hill.pdf

EO Basics. (n.d.). Retrieved July 9, 2014, from Essential Oils for Dummies: http://www.essentialoilsfordummys.com/p/essential-oil-basics_26.html

Hauck, D. W. (n.d.). *The History of Essential Oils.* Retrieved June 29, 2014, from Crucible: http://www.crucible.org/oils_history.htm

Science Definition. (n.d.). Retrieved July 14, 2014, from Science Made Simple: http://www.sciencemadesimple.com/science-definition.html

Scientific Advisory Board. (n.d.). Retrieved July 15, 2014, from doTERRA: http://www.doterra.com/us/companyScientificAdvisoryBoard.php

What Is an Essential Oil? (n.d.). Retrieved July 10, 2014, from doTERRA: http://www.doterra.com/us/essentialDefinition.php

CPSIA information can be obtained at www.ICGtesting.com
Printed in the USA
LVOW09s2328110416

483163LV00019B/230/P

9 781505 365795